If you want to learn how to make a Branded Book
of your own then go to this link

https://payhip.com/b/MH3A

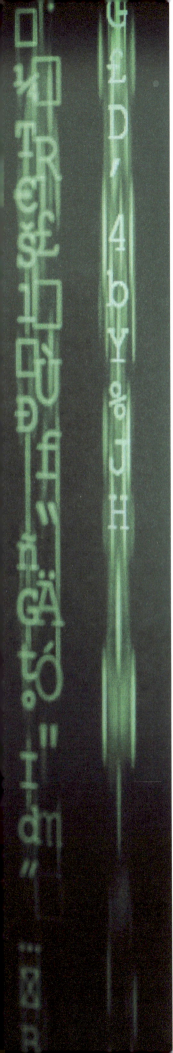

Table Of Contents

How Safe is Your Digital World?

When a data breach occurs at a mighty conglomerate it's all over the news and social media but what happens when it's an attack against the little guy?

A report by cyber security firm Symantec stated that over half of the cyber-attacks world-wide in 2015 (43%) were against small businesses, because attackers see small businesses as an easy or soft target. You need the basic know-how to protect your digital self and that's what this book aims to do.

In this book, over 10 lessons over days, you will learn about; the main types of attacks that impact on small businesses, how to spot them, how to pro-actively protect your digital self and what to do if you are the victim of an attack.

Introduction

Introduction

Thanks for being brave enough to step into the world of cyber security, you won't regret it, even though the very wording can cause the most tech savvy person a certain amount of unease or anxiety.

I'm Cat and I'll be your guide for this book. I won't baffle you with science or set out to scare you (that's for Halloween!). I will however make this as straight forward and easy to understand as humanly possible.

I used to head up intelligence analysis for a national enforcement agency, as well as doing loads of other stuff, so I promise, you're in a safe pair of hands.

In this short 10 lesson book you are going to learn the basics of cyber security, the types of information you need to think about securing and most importantly, how to take really easy practical steps to secure your digital everything.

You might be here because you've already had your website or email attacked or hacked but hopefully you're here before that happens.

I'll explain the basics of the steps you can take to stop future attacks in their tracks and by the end of this book you will have a good knowledge of what steps to take right now to reduce your chances of being attacked in the first place and secure your digital self.

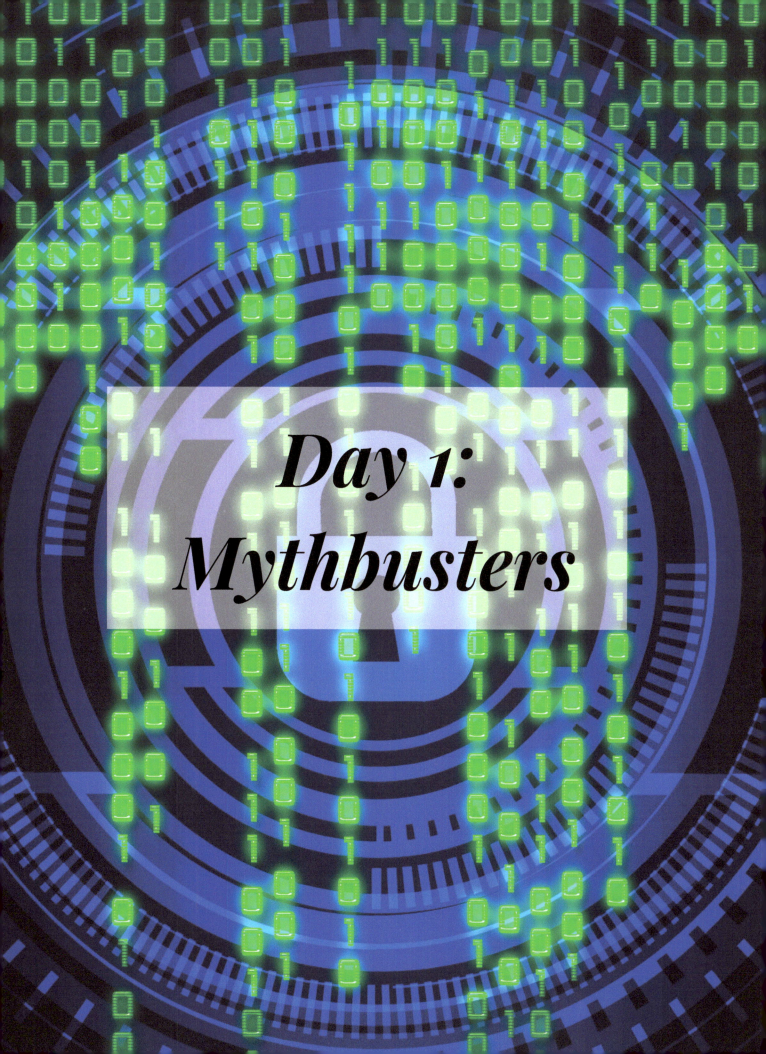

Day 1:
Mythbusters

MYTH BUSTERS

1 Cyber attacks are reserved solely for the big corporations or blue chip companies.

Wrong!
Whilst those attacks make a compelling headline, in actual fact, small businesses have become the latest sector to fall onto attackers hit lists.

Why? Because small businesses have many digital assets to protect but very limited funds and know-how to secure them effectively.
https://www.towergateinsurance.co.uk/liability-insurance/smes-and-cyber-attacks.

2 I don't collect or hold any customer details on my website and use third party email automation or CRM software so I'm not a target".

Wrong!
Your website is not just a target for customer information, this is just one type of attack. Your site can be used as a host for attacks on other sites effectively becoming a robot working for nefarious ends for the cyber criminal or the aim is to damage your professional reputation.

3 I only use secure networks or my phone providers data roaming while surfing in public places so I'm pretty safe.

Take Note!
Widespread use of mobile devices and accessing the internet in public places has seen cyber criminals adapt their attacking technique to exploit the vulnerabilities in the phone software or WiFi/data connection in public spaces.

MYTH BUSTERS

4 I use a mac which can't get infected.

Wrong!
Whilst mac's have a different operating system they are not immune and can easily still pass on viruses to other computers.

Don't panic if you silently nodded along with all of some of the myths and are now thinking...what the heck do I do?

Keep going, follow the lessons and you'll be more cyber savvy in 10 short days!

In the next lesson we are going to start looking at some common cyber security attacks that affect small businesses.

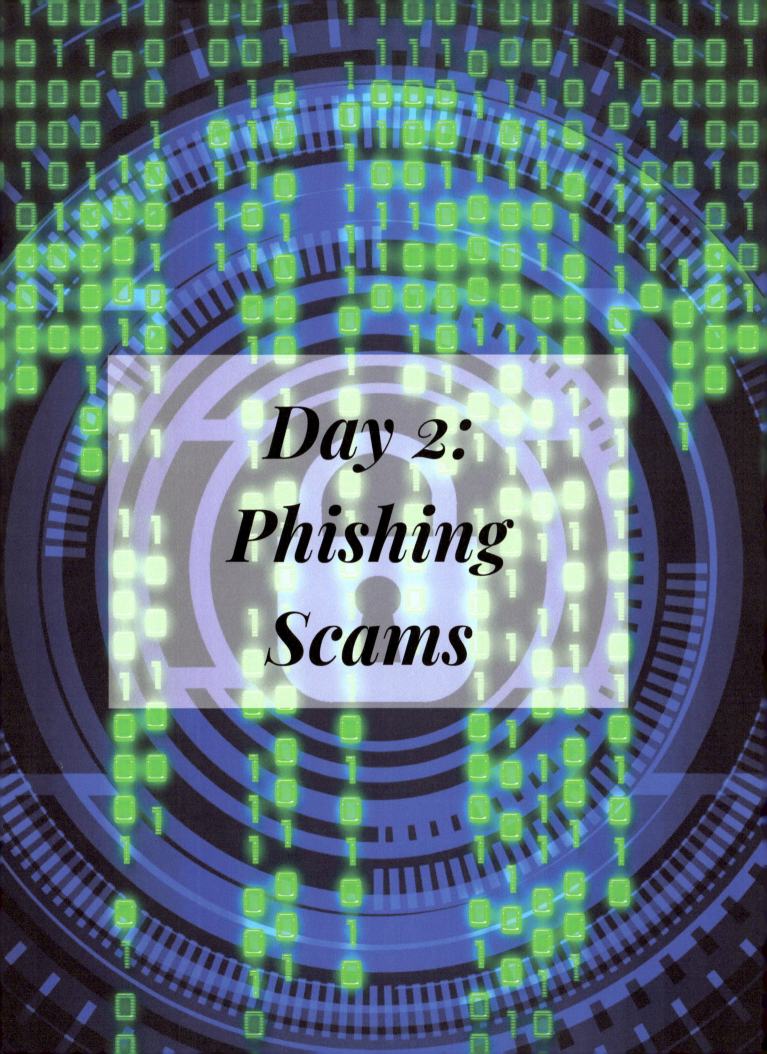

Day 2:
Phishing
Scams

Day 2: Phishing Scams

PHISHING SCAM

Phishing is when emails, phone calls or websites purport to be a person or organisation that you trust with the sole aim of gaining your personal information such as; passwords, account details or credit card numbers.

Essentially, phishing is social engineering where a feeling of trust is created through psychological manipulation and exploiting human weakness to steal your personal information.

Most of these attacks are subtle, an email message alerting you to an unpaid bill or security breach, a reminder to pay an invoice and asking you to follow the link in the email to solve the problem immediately.

Other types of phishing attacks are more aggressive, with cyber criminals lifting personal information you may have made, accidently or otherwise, available publicly through social media channels.

Day 2: Phishing Scams Contd.

SPEAR PHISHING SCAM

Is also a common type of attack against small businesses, with a specific targeted objective when sending emails to company employees purporting to be from a trusted partner and therefore more likely to be opened.

Here are some examples;

- Wishing your mum a happy 50th wedding anniversary with comments about her maiden name. A cyber criminal just loves this type of information as lots of old security questions use 'mothers' maiden name' as a security check on credit cards or bank details.

- Posting pictures of your favourite pet along with its name on social media channels and you happen to use this in a password that you use across several of your on-line logins for your personal and/or business digital life .

- A phone call telling you that your PC firewall is out of date or expiring and a discounted price to install new security software if bought there and then.

- An employee posting data on social media that provides company information as part of a social engineering scam.

- An email to the company stating they are from your company bank or other trusted partner and an employee clicks on the link.

Day 2: Phishing Scams Contd.

PROTECT YOURSELF AND YOUR BUSINESS

- Bad grammar or spelling mistakes are common in emails that are part of a phishing .scam

- Suspicious links in emails can be checked by hovering your mouse pointer over the link without clicking. You can see where the link leads and it more often than not won't match the text in the link within the email. Don't click!

- If the message in the email creates a sense of threat and urgency there is a good chance that it is a phishing scam.

- Email addresses that look like they are from trusted organisations but on closer inspection have a slightly different look. An additional letter or spelling is altered.

- Treat all unsolicited phone calls with skepticism and suspicion. Most big companies will not cold call you.

- If unsolicited phone calls have an element of threat and urgency, again hang up immediately.

- Create awareness for all employees about spear phishing scams. This could be added to the company induction pack or briefing.

REPORT EVERYTHING AND ANYTHING SUSPICIOUS

Phishing scam emails can usually reported within your email provider by dropping them in the junk or spam folder then having the option to 'report', block and delete.

If you can record a phone callers information you can report it to the relevant authorities:

- U.S.A. - FTC Complaint Commission
  https://www.ftccomplaintassistant.gov/#crnt&panel1-1

- U.K. - Action Fraud
  http://www.actionfraud.police.uk OR

  Register your number to prevent cold calls TPS online
  http://www.tpsonline.org.uk/tps/index.html

- Canada - Canadian Anti-Fraud Centre
  http://www.antifraudcentre- centreantifraude.ca/index-eng.htm

In the next lesson, I'll introduce you to malware attacks, what they are and what to do about them.

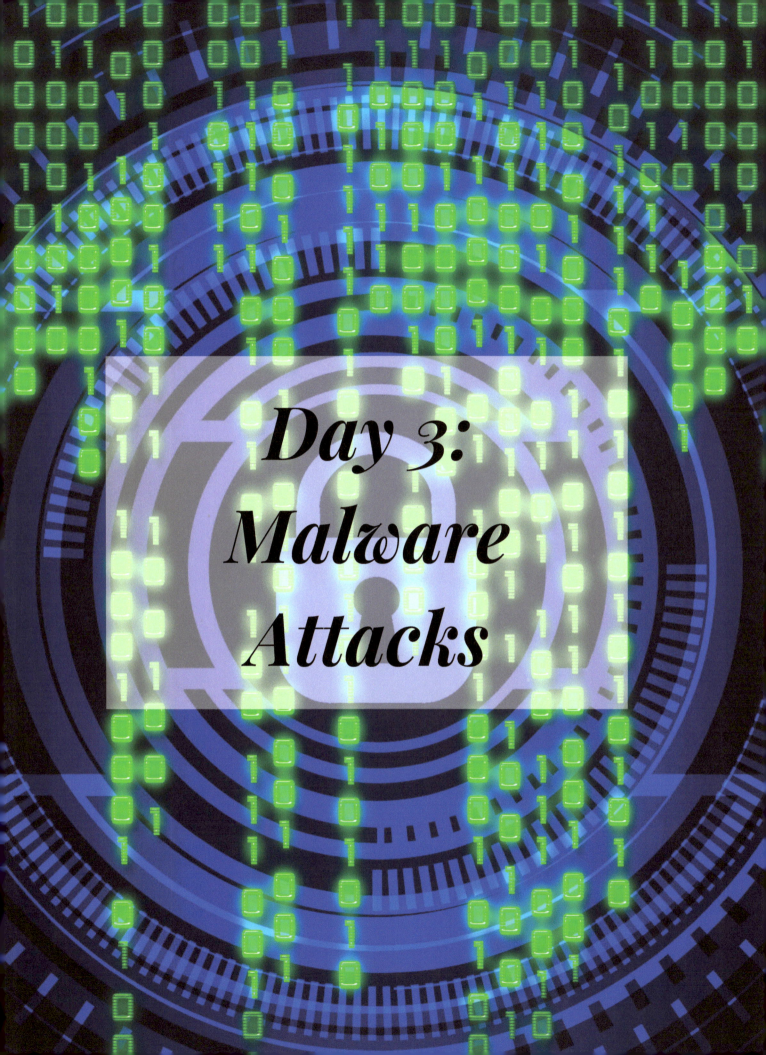

Day 3: Malware Attacks

Day 3: Malware Attacks

MALWARE

This is primarily a collective term used to refer to a variety of forms of hostile or intrusive software including; computer viruses, worms, trojan horses, ransomware, spyware and other malicious programs.

It can take the form of executable code, scripts, active content, and other software.

Here's a bit more explanation of these types of malware;

- Viruses, worms and trojan horses – in layman's terms are pieces of malicious code used to infect your PC or laptop:

  - Viruses are usually attached to a file (e.g. exe executable file) which when passed between computers by email but only damage files if executed (clicked on).

  - Worms are malicious code that can travel without human interaction via information sharing on your system.

  - Trojan horses – Looks innocent enough like useful software but once downloaded can delete files or damage your operating system.

  - Ransomware – Your digital data or access is effectively held to ransom until a payment is made to the criminal.

  - Botnets – Your PC or laptop is used as part of a group of computers to bombard another website with spam emails or huge amounts of data with the intent of putting the website temporarily out of commission or to steal personal information on a large scale.

  - Spyware – Software that records the activities of the PC or laptop user, recording keystrokes used for login and password access.

Day 3: Malware Attacks Contd.

PROTECT YOURSELF AND YOUR BUSINESS

- Keep your operating system updated. Yes I know it can be annoying when you're slaving away, you've got a deadline to hit and you just know that by hitting the 'run update now' option will make sure you need to step away from your laptop for anything between 10mins and 24hrs.

  If you continue to postpone updates however, every minute that it is not run is another minute something can go spectacularly wrong and cause permanent damage or at least an irritating longer period of downtime. If you have no I.T department and are flying solo, this is even more important!

- Install a firewall on your system. I would recommend installing a software firewall on your PC. This will shut down external attempts to access or control your computer. You can install hardware firewalls on your router too to protect the network as software firewalls will only protect the PC it is loaded onto. MACs don't always have firewalls activated by default so make sure to check your security settings.

- Keep your firewall software updated. Just like the operating system to make sure all current threats are addressed the software is continually updated by the owners/creator so you need to keep it updated too.

- Get rid of or update old software on your system. If you have old software on your system that is no longer supported by the owner and therefore is not being updated get rid of it otherwise it creates a vulnerability, a route for attackers to exploit. If it has an update you haven't yet run, run the update!

- Install anti-virus software on your PC. There are loads of free anti-virus software versions out there with the option to buy upgrades for specific purposes. Run these regularly or allow them to automatically update for ongoing anti-virus protection on your system.

Day 4: Password Attacks

PASSWORD ATTACK

This is exactly what it says on the tin, an attack on yours or your employees' passwords to gain wider access to your system(s).

These types of attacks are usually classed as brute force attacks where the attacker uses a piece of software that will continually try random passwords, in a trial and error approach, in an attempt to crack your code and break into your system.

Brute force attacks are common on websites where attackers attempt to gain access to the back-end of your website in order to delete files, inflict damage to files or re- direct your website to another destination or use as a robot for a wider campaign or attack.

If an attacker gains entry due to weak passwords even if you don't hold customer or client data on your site, they can do untold reputational damage. It's not the first time I've tried to access a site only to find a porn site pop up in it's place.

Even if you get back control of your site and domain name, do you think potential customers who experienced the re-direct would come back to your site?

The impact and cost of changing your brand, domain names and fixing your reputation are essentially priceless.

Can you afford not to be proactive in protecting your digital world?

Day 4: Password Attacks Contd.

PROTECT YOURSELF AND YOUR BUSINESS

- Strong passwords. Avoid the use of passwords that use actual dictionary words or only lower case letters. These types of passwords are just making it easy for attackers to mount a brute force attack. A weak password is the equivalent of leaving your keys hanging in the lock.

- Replacing passwords regularly. Regularly switching and changing passwords is good practice to ensure a higher level of security for your digital world. Ok, I know it is so difficult to remember every single password for every single program or app that you access but what is the cost of not putting this practice in place?

- Use a password manager. A good way to avoid having to remember 100's of passwords where the temptation arises to duplicate or write them down, a good password manager is a great choice.

  There are loads to choose from. My personal favourite is LastPass. You are only required to remember one master password and it locks all your passwords for every site you log deep in it's secure vaults. You can run security checks from time to time to check for weaknesses and vulnerabilities and schedule password changes that it remembers for you. It can also be used across multiple sites and devices on their paid options which is a must.

- Beware of disgruntled employees. Ensure you have a practice in place to remove access rights and passwords from any employees leaving your employment. It's not the first time I've seen disgruntled employees change all passwords to business social media accounts and they continue to post under the name of the organisation – you can imagine...carnage! Again, a password manager can assist you with this in a small business where you can automatically remove a person's access rights as and when you need to

In the next lesson we are going to look at Denial of Service Attacks.

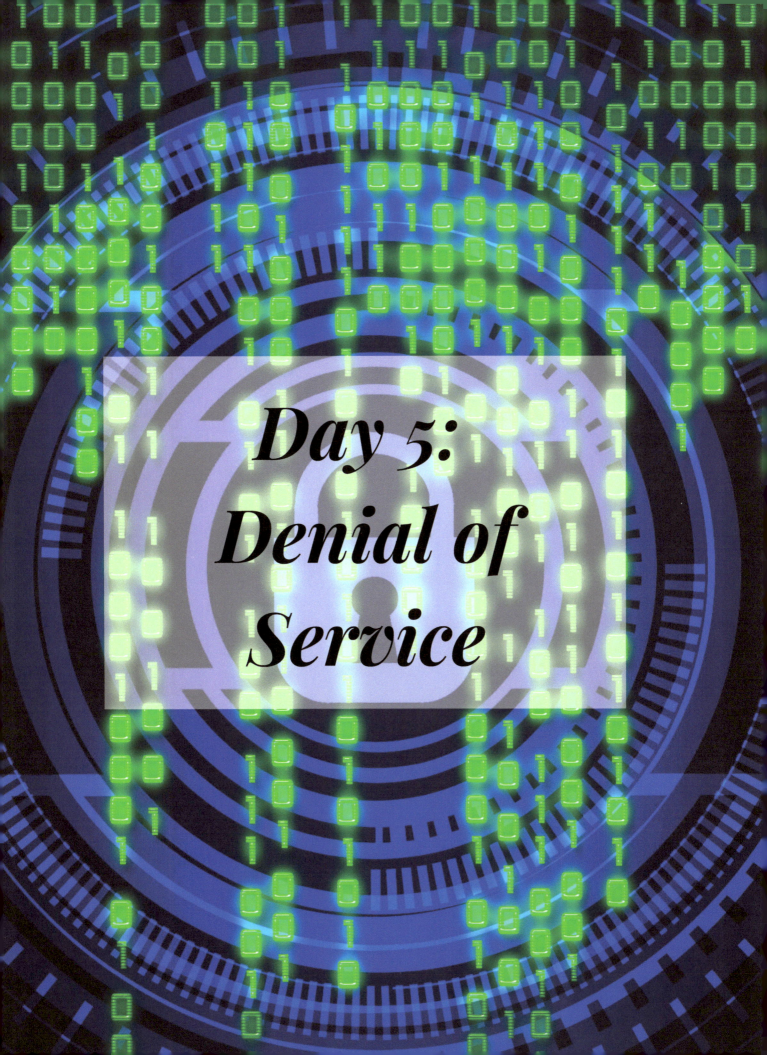

Day 5:
Denial of
Service

Day 5: Denial of Service

DENIAL OF SERVICE (DoS) ATTACKS

A denial of service attack aims to disrupt a whole network where attackers send a high volume of traffic and data to a site with the sole purpose of overloading the system with huge amounts of connection requests.

It's like trying to pour more and more water into a balloon (I'm sure you still have water fights) until it can hold no more and it bursts.

For this to work effectively the attacker will have 'recruited' a high volume of computers, unknown to the users, to contribute to the high volume attack.

This type of attack effectively turns your PC into a zombie working on behalf of the attacker.

Your own computer may even have contributed to a DoS attack that hit the news without you even knowing!

Day 5: Denial of Service Contd.

PROTECT YOURSELF AND YOUR BUSINESS

Unless your business is growing you will probably not be on the receiving end of a DoS attack however your personal and business computer could be easily used in an attack.

- Audit your internet traffic. Are there any weird or unusual spikes in traffic that you can't account for? This could point to a DoS attack.

- Has your company been involved in any polarising political movement. The focus of DoS attacks are highly likely to be motivated to shut down commercial sites, usually paired with a ransom demand to get your site up and running again.

- Keep your anti-virus, firewalls and computer software updated. Any cracks in your armour can be exploited. You can also visit the Microsoft or Apple sites for current threats to make sure you are protected as far as possible.

In the next lesson we are going to look at why you need to protect your personal and business data whilst surfing on a public WiFi connection.

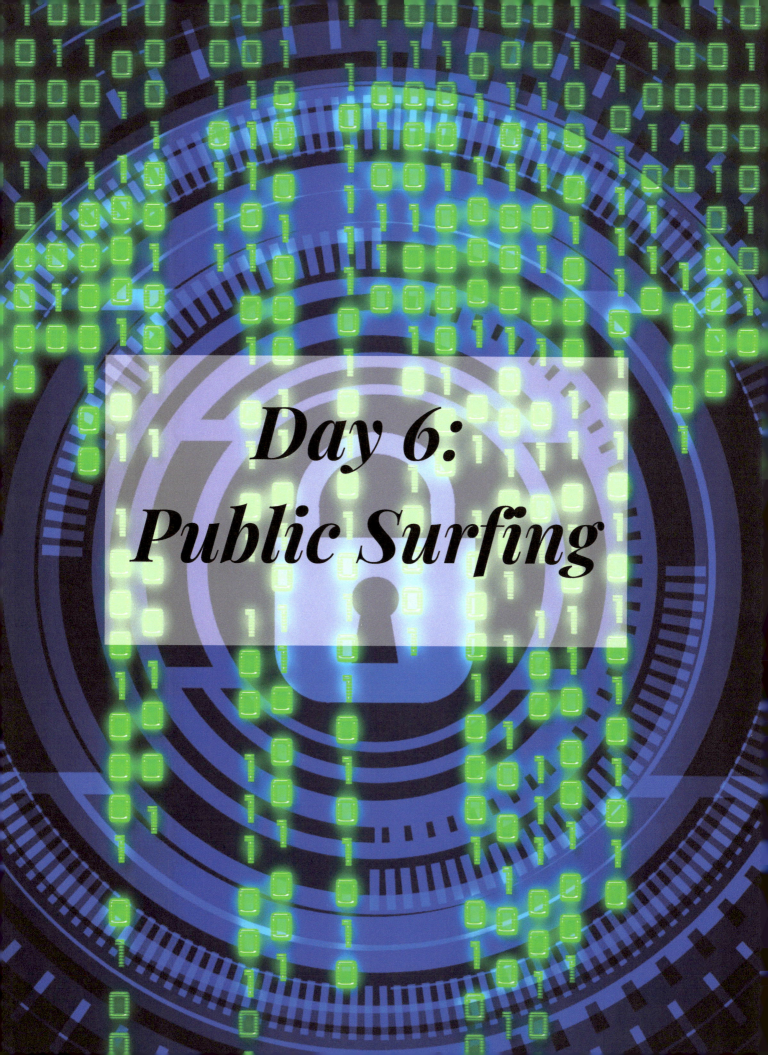

Day 6:
Public Surfing

PUBLIC SURFING

We are in an age of being able to work from literally anywhere in the world. If you have a laptop, smartphone or tablet and a WiFi connection we can be connected right across the globe in a nanosecond (I'm currently updating this book from a cafe in Marrakech).

The coffee shops are rammed with loads of shiny laptop gazers, sipping on lattes or having loud conversations on their phones, without thought or worry about what sensitive information they are potentially sharing publicly.

It's liberating for the small business owner who no longer has to endure a hard wired internet connection to get their work done.

They can pack up their wireless kit and work; on trains, in airports, in coffee shops or wherever they can get a half decent WiFi connection. The world is their oyster (or connected cafe however you want to see it).

The problem is that there are some not-so-nice people in this world who are quite willing to use these public WiFi spaces to exploit and steal private information for nefarious ends.

Every smart-phone, tablet or laptop user in a public space is subjecting their personal information to considerable risk because of ease that data that can be intercepted through public WiFi networks.

We are getting better at knowing we need anti-virus software and firewalls on our computers but do we even think about the risks of checking in on Facebook or checking our email, probably not.

I don't know about you but I don't want to give up the convenience of accessing public WiFi in shopping malls, airports or cafes just because there are some unscrupulous people in the world just lying in wait to steal our personal data. So what can you do to protect your digital world in a public space?

Day 6: Public Surfing Contd.

PROTECT YOURSELF AND YOUR BUSINESS

- Public WiFi is insecure. As soon as you log onto public WiFi you are exposing yourself to a potential threat. Ensure that you connect to the correct connection. Many attackers set up bogus connections that look like the cafe or mall to get you to click.

- All devices are at risk. Your phone and tablet are still powerful computers that hold a lot of data when connected to the internet. Treat them no different from your computer – the risks are the same. Install and keep updated anti-virus software on your phone to scan and clean potential threats.

- Don't connect to sensitive sites in public spaces. If you are browsing in public spaces don't connect to online banking or sites that have stored your credit card details. These are at higher risk of exposure and attack.

- Ensure your own network settings are set for public network i.e. to keep it safe whilst connected to a public network without sharing files or being visible. Whilst your computer may be virus free, by connecting to a public network you could be infected or compromised by other infected devices that are connected to the public network.

You can also install a Virtual Private Network (VPN) which will be explained in the next lesson.

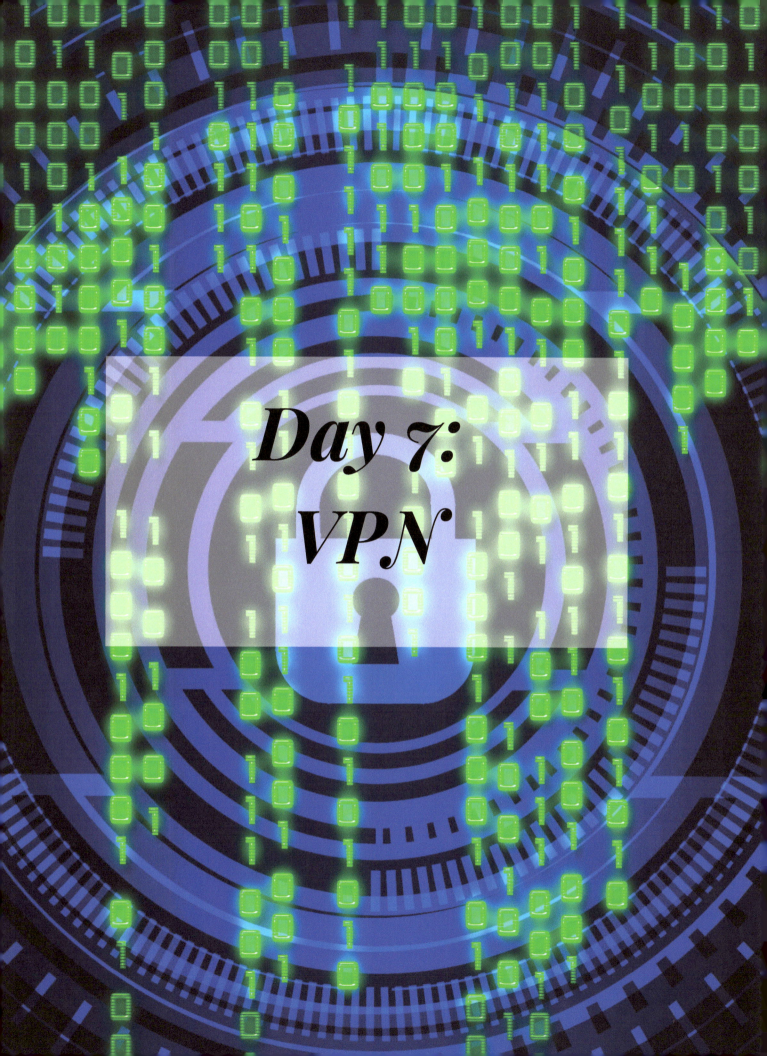

Day 7:
VPN

Day 7: Virtual Private Network

VIRTUAL PRIVATE NETWORK (VPN)

In layman's terms a VPN is snazzy bit of tech that creates a private and encrypted secure connection over an insecure network.

You set up and connect through a private network which blocks anyone from seeing what you are doing online.

A potential attacker may be able to see that you are connected to a private network but can't see your activity or break through the barrier of the private network.

It's like having your own bubble of armour that protects your data when you are browsing or accessing the internet in public spaces.

Again, there are a number of virtual private networks to choose from. A good way to start assessing what type of VPN you need is to compare the benefits and features to your own personal and company requirements.

Is it just you or do you have sales people who are out and about – this can make a difference in cost and type.

Day 7: VPN Contd.

VIRTUAL PRIVATE NETWORK (VPN) BENEFITS

Here are some of the benefits of different VPN products that you should consider;

- A VPN can be installed and used across multiple devices ensuring you are protected at all times.

- Some VPNs use bank-grade encryption, keeping you super safe when surfing the net.

- Browse anonymously and keep your activity private from prying eyes.

- Some VPNs offer by-passing of geo-restricted content so you can literally move your IP address (unique address that identifies your computer) to look like you are browsing from another country at the flip of a switch.

- Block and intercept annoying cookie data that normally follows you around the internet (sick of that ad that pops up after you browsed Amazon? Some VPNs can block this activity).

- Check that the VPN provider isn't logging your information on their system.

I recommend IP Vanish as my VPN provider of choice. I can use it across multiple devices, including mobiles, laptop and Amazon Fire Stick. They are budget friendly but don't compromise on security. Go to https://straighttalkingginger.com/stuff-i-use to get a deal on a starter account with IP Vanish.

In the next lesson we are going to look at how to choose a secure host provider for your website so that you know your gorgeous site is as secure as it can be.

Day 8:
Secure Hosting

Day 8: Secure Hosting

SECURE HOSTING

Quite simply, you cannot afford to ignore the security of your website.

In earlier lessons you learned that sites can be compromised by brute force attacks and redirected to less scrupulous site that could permanently damage your company reputation, your brand and the inner workings of your site.

One of the key considerations when setting up a website is the hosting provider and their attitude and logistics to secure your data.

Too often we can be tempted to go for the cheapest hosting option as a small business owner, only considering band-with, expense, the fact a domain name or site builder is thrown into the package, but maybe not fully understanding the security implications and impact longer term if a compromise was to happen.

On day 10 you will get a list of really helpful resources which includes a thorough explanation of the considerations around hosting but for today's lesson, and to get you moving (and comparing host providers)...

Day 8: Secure Hosting Contd.

SECURE HOSTING – QUESTIONS TO ASK A HOST:

1. Does the host provider have a security policy? A number of providers provide the band-with and server space leaving security up to you however you don't know, what you don't know and it may not have been on your radar to secure your site.

2. How do the host provider protect their own network? After all, if they are compromised, you are compromised.

3. If something goes wrong what actions do they take to protect your data and get your site back up and running? What are the timescales for this? This is particularly important as a small business owner with an eCommerce site. You're not making sales while your site is down.

4. Does your provider provide you with an SSL certificate as part of their package? This is important for the security of customers purchasing through your website. You want their data transactions to be secure and encrypted. Google ranking requires an SSL certificate.

5. Who is responsible for updating software and other applications? If the host are responsible make sure you see it in a contract. If not, you'll need to start thinking about finding a knowledgeable website developer or security expert to keep you safe. We all have a plumber or electrician in our phone book, it's time to add a developer to the contact list.

6. What is your on-going security monitoring policy? This could be regular malware checks, firewall checks, blacklist of suspicious IP addresses or activity.

These are good starting points for considering your security options. If it was a brick and mortar business you would make sure there was; an alarm, CCTV or shutters and if the shop window was broken, you'd have the glass repairer out in a flash.

Your website is your online shop front - it needs to be just as secure.

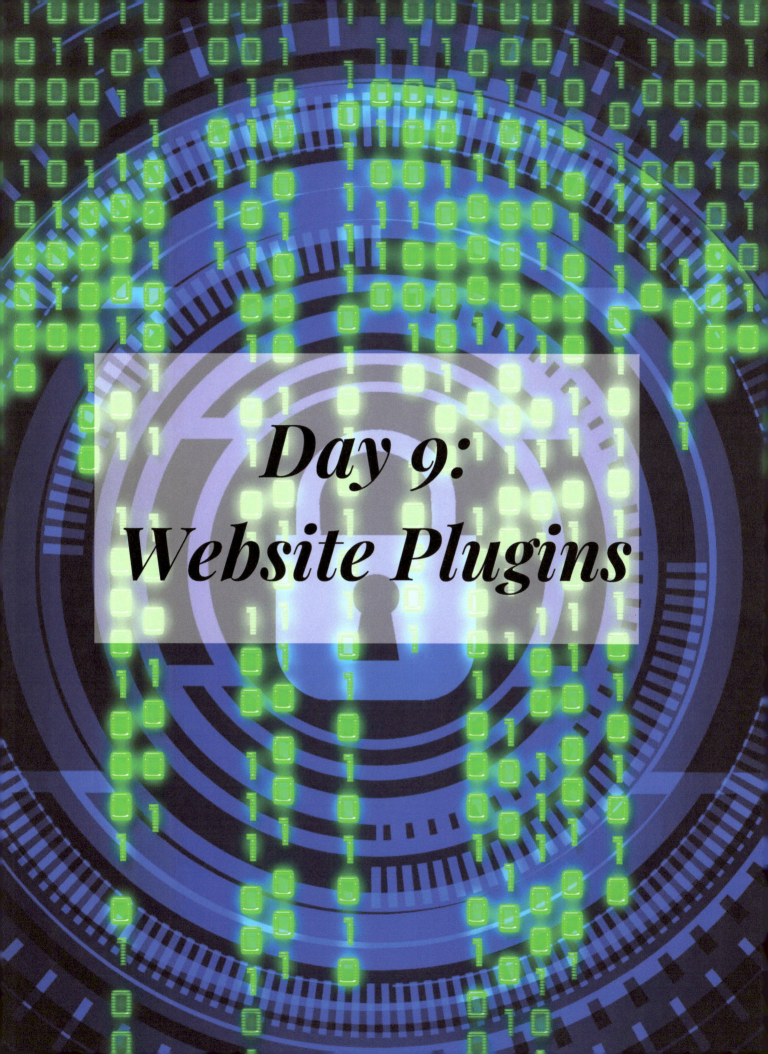

Day 9:
Website Plugins

Day 9: Website Plugins

WORDPRESS WEBSITE PLUGINS

If you're a WordPress user you'll know that there are literally 100's of website plug- ins to choose from, almost verging on kid in a sweet shop level of awe, with the shiny object syndrome tugging on your magpie instincts with tremendous strength.

But just before you go and buy up every plug-in without thought, plan or strategy just take a moment to think about security and the potential problems you may face.

It's well known that your site can suffer big time if you install far too many plug-ins simultaneously, never mind the hit on your bank balance, with the maximum recommended number of plug-ins being between 10 and 12 installed and in operation at any one time.

There's another consideration, yep you guessed it, how secure is your new plug-in going to be?

Day 9: Website Plugins Contd.

WORDPRESS WEBSITE PLUGINS

Due to the very nature of plug-ins some can be far less secure than others. I admit there is no fool proof method for spotting an insecure plug-in but you can mitigate some of the risk by doing as follows:

PLUG-IN SECURITY CHECK-LIST

☐ What do you need in a plug-in? Instead of buying 2 or 3 would 1 do the job?

☐ Check the reviews carefully. If a plug-in is rated 4 or 5 stars but there are only 2 reviews, it might be best to step away and find an alternative until you have more details.

☐ Google the name of the plug-in with the wording 'security' or 'vulnerabilities'. Anything that is of concern should be flagged up in a Google search: "[plugin name] + security".

☐ Check when the owner last updated the plug-in - the last month is a good rule of thumb. If they no longer support it there are guaranteed to be holes in their code that haven't been patched against the latest threats and it may no longer be compatible with WordPress.

☐ Take the time to read the comments as I find that users are fairly honest and vocal online if they hit any issues.

Day 9: Website Plugins Contd.

SQUARESPACE

If you are a Squarespace user, all of the hosting and security is handled by the team at Squarespace. There are no plug-ins to worry about or conflicting software, it's all built and tested by their in-house team.

The most common breach type of Squarespace sites is by disgruntled employees or Website developers who for one reason or another have not had their access rights removed at the end of employment or end of client agreement and have made changes without the permission of the owner.

There are measures that can easily be put into place to stop this type of activity before untold damage is done.

You can report Squarespace vulnerabilitities here: https://www.squarespace.com/security

In the next and final lesson, you will learn about website back-up and get a load of additional resource links to further your knowledge.

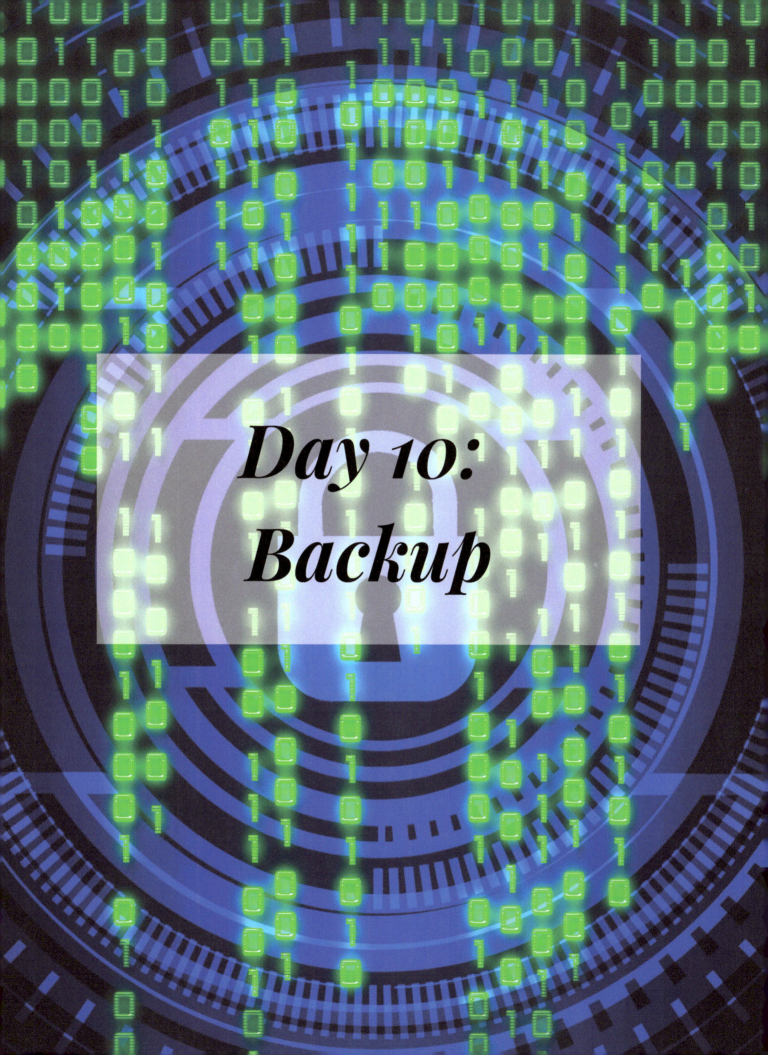

Day 10:
Backup

WEBSITE BACK-UP

It's all going swimmingly, you have a gorgeous website, there's a steady stream of traffic and boom you delete a bit of code by mistake, you've missed a critical WordPress update, malware has infected your site or you're in the middle of moving hosts (now you've found a more secure site) and your lovely website has suddenly up and disappeared.

But it's OK because you regularly back-up your site, don't you?

A bit like finding a secure host, you don't know what you don't know and often regular back-ups are an overlooked part of owning and operating a successful and secure website.

Back-ups are an essential part of maintenance but because, thankfully, you won't need to use them that often it doesn't mean you shouldn't make it a regular task.

No website is immune from a bit of technical drama now and again.

I would recommend backing up daily, especially if you have loads of traffic to your site or make changes regularly. At a minimum this should be done monthly for site files and weekly for database files but certainly straight after you have made any change such as; posted a blog or changed some code if you're a bit more website savvy.

Back-ups should also be done prior to installing a new version of WordPress so if anything at all goes awry you can slide back to a previous version.

Day 10: Backup + Other Stuff Contd.

WEBSITE BACK-UP

There are loads of ways to perform back-ups, there are plug-ins galore, some more technical than others.

Here are some considerations when thinking about a method of back-up:

- Can the back-up be automated so you can set it and forget it, especially to fit in with a regular schedule?

- Does the back-up get automatically stored in dropbox or other cloud storage provider for ease of access? If it's only held by the web host provider and they get hacked you've got a problem. It's best to store back-ups elsewhere.

- Can the back-up be easily restored? It's all very well backing up the files but can they be re-installed and restored easily.

- Consider using an online service that performs the back-up and stores your data for a monthly fee or...

- Use a WordPress plug-in that performs scheduled back-ups and stores them in cloud storage.

By this point you should have a bit more savvy around your security and either feel calm that you've got it in hand or now have a checklist of things you need to go and do immediately.

Thanks for taking the time to go through these lessons and congratulations on getting your digital world secure!

Bonus
Resources

RESOURCES

If you want to get into more of the detail about cyber security then the Sophos Threatsaurus is a must read. It literally covers every term from A - Z relevant to cyber security.
https://www.sophos.com/en-us/security-news-trends/security-trends/threatsaurus.aspx

Apple publish their current security updates here:
https://www.apple.com/support/security

Windows publish their current security updates here:
https://technet.microsoft.com/en-us/security/dn440717

How to choose between a hardware firewall and software firewall:
http://home.mcafee.com/advicecenter/?id=ad_ost_hvsf&ctst=1

How to choose a hosting provider:
 https://www.sophos.com/en-us/security-news-trends/security- trends/choosing-a-hosting-provider.aspx#

www.ingramcontent.com/pod-product-compliance
Lightning Source LLC
Chambersburg PA
CBHW041432050326

40690CB00002B/511